2RRO2R

the notebook edition

Colour the Classics
xoxo

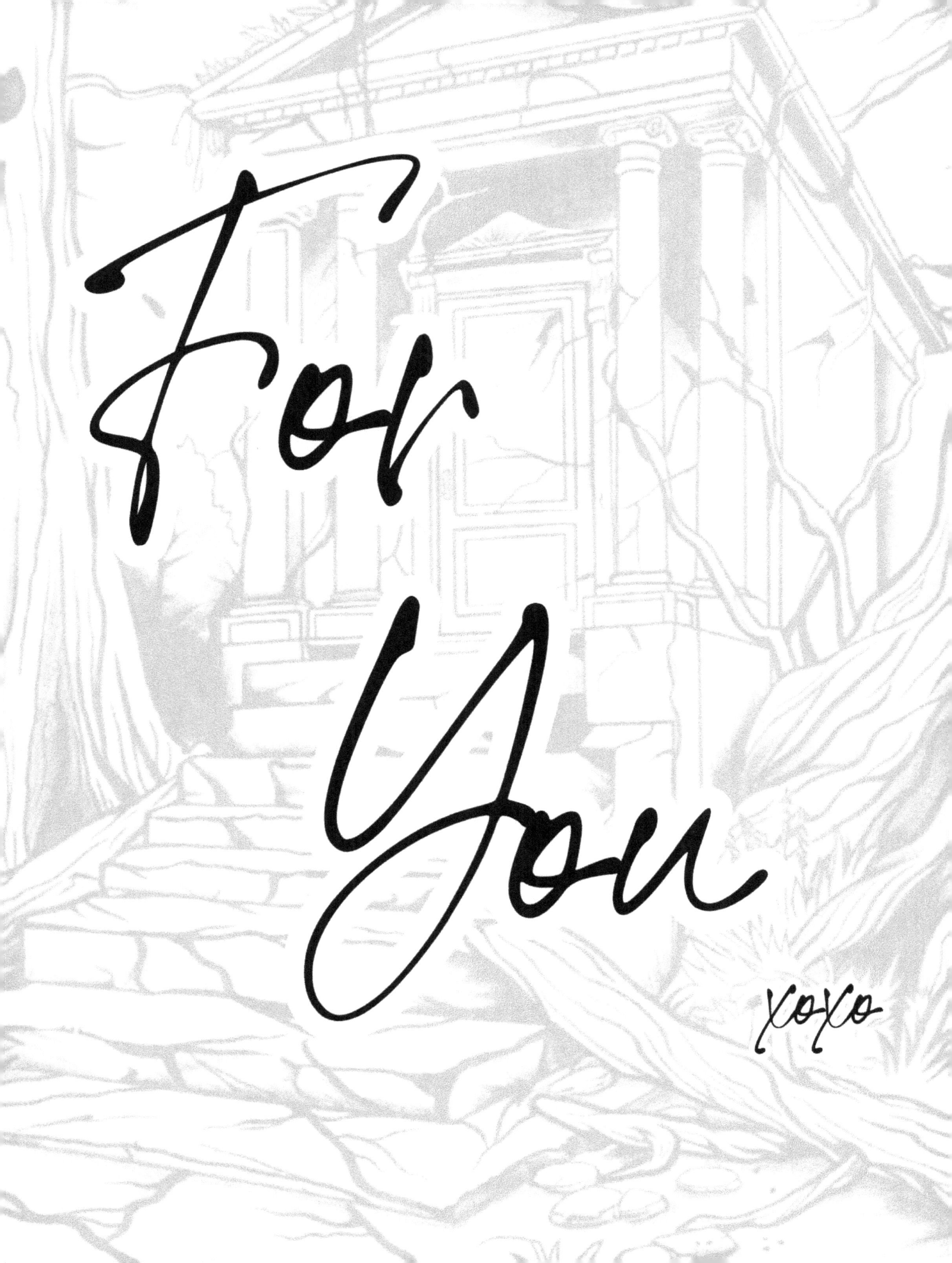For You
xoxo

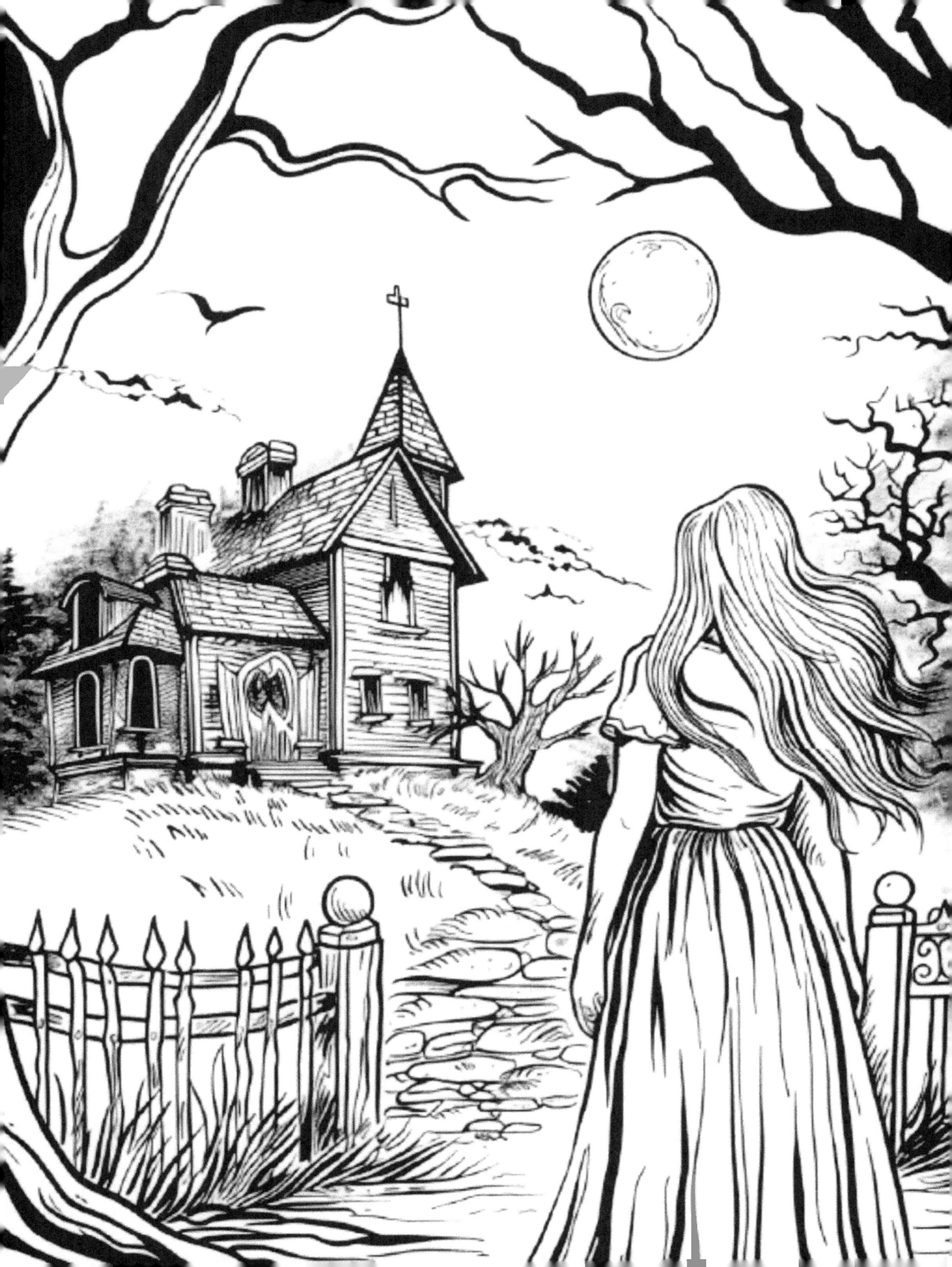

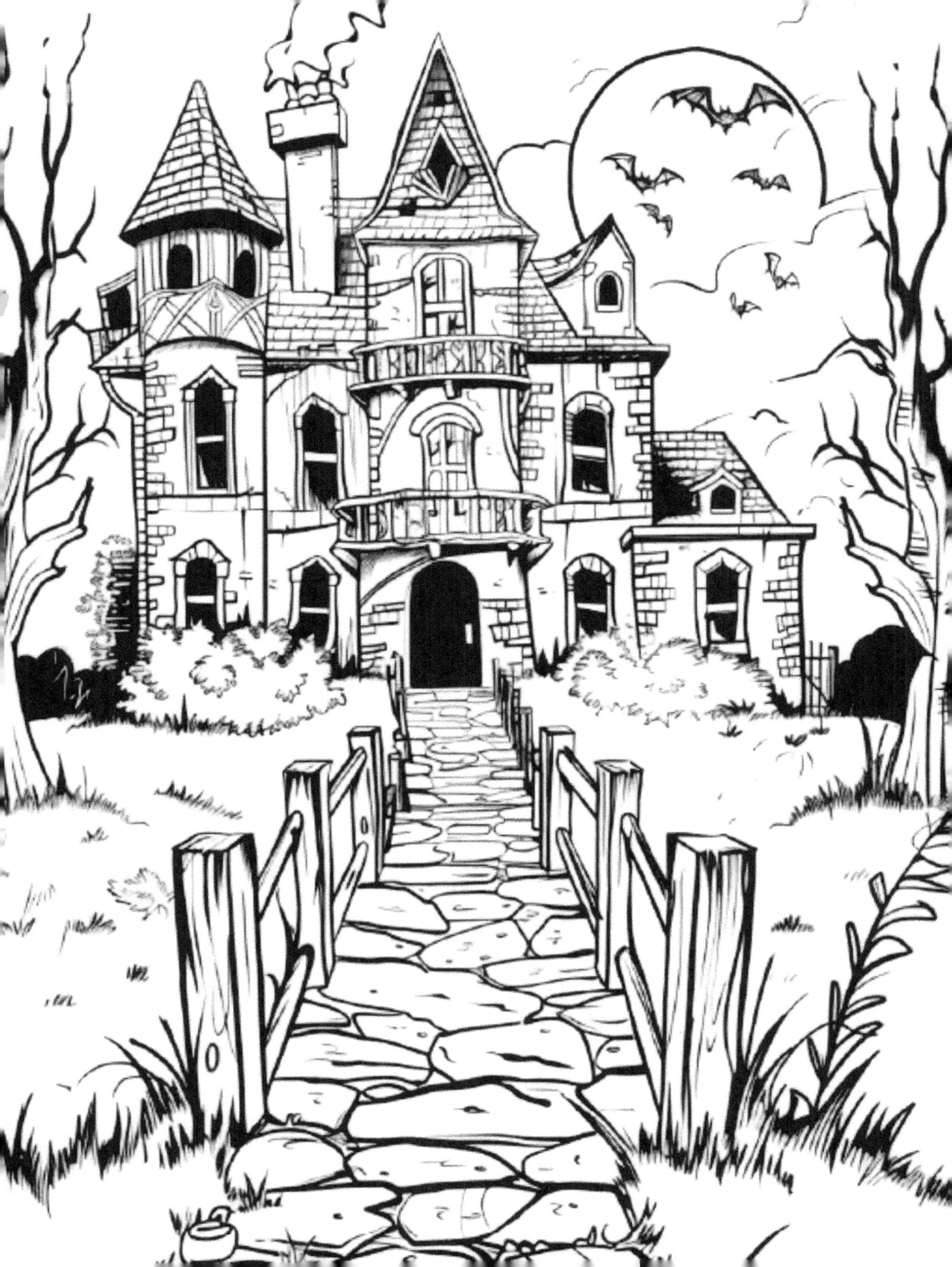

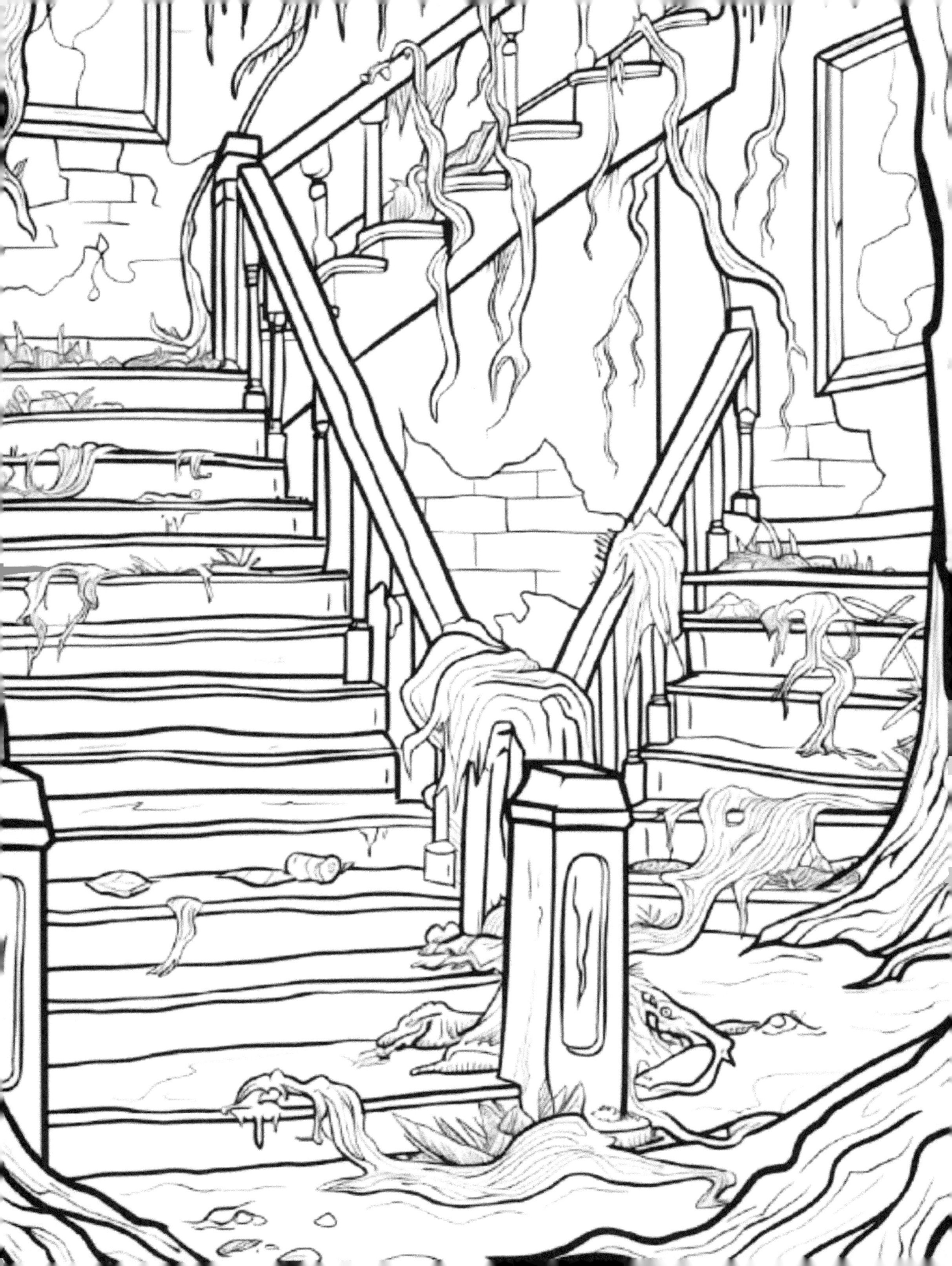

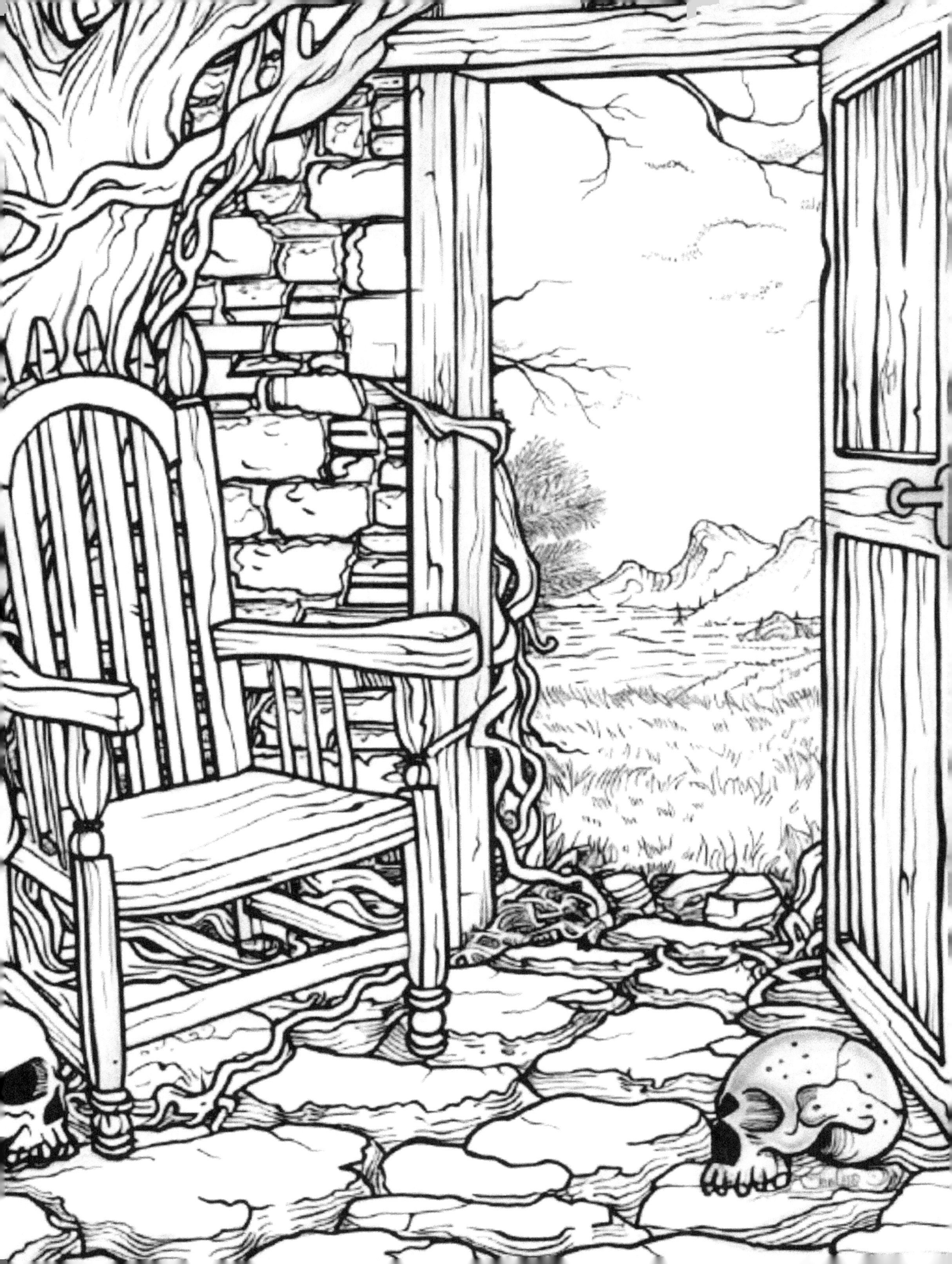

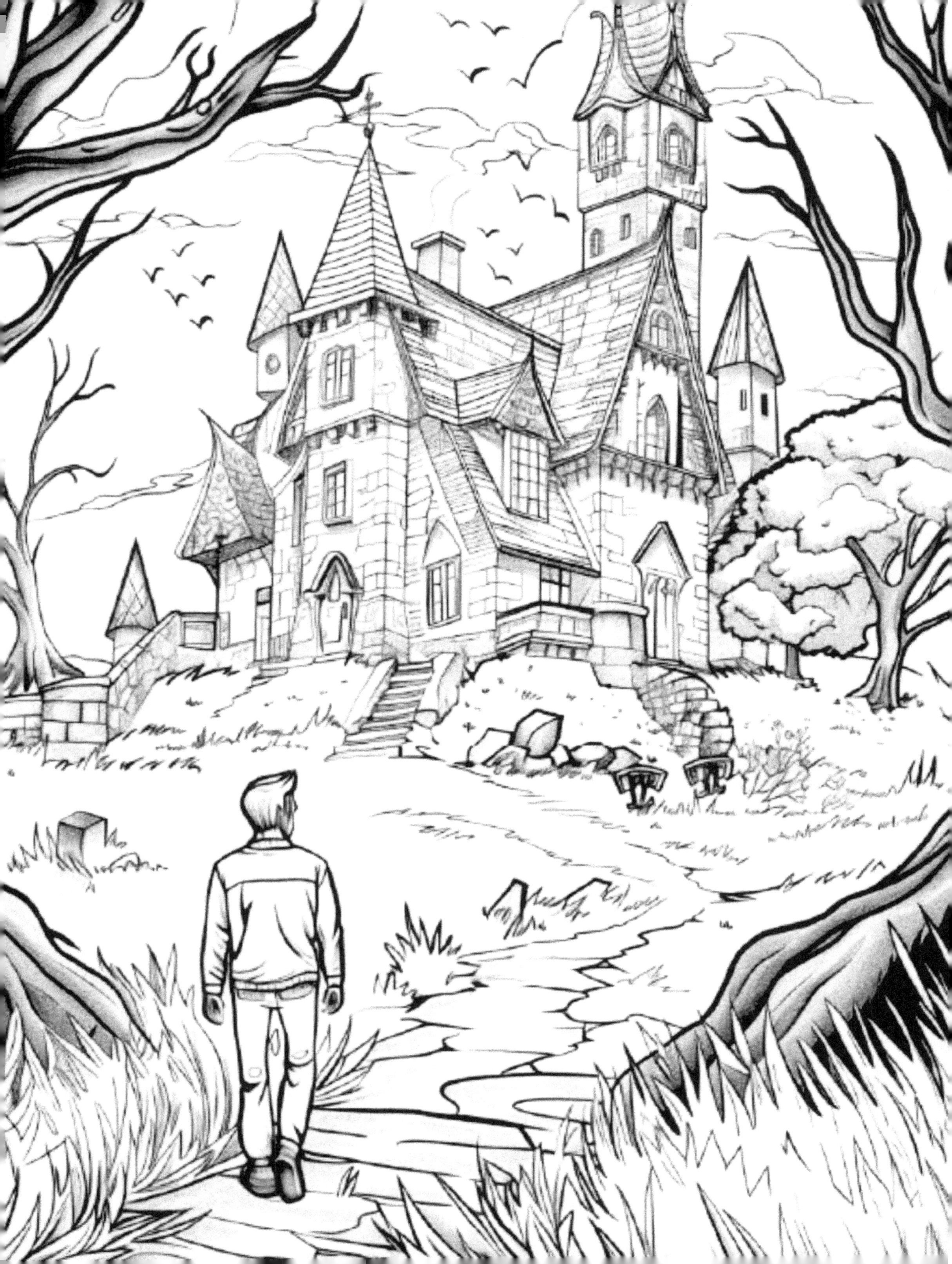

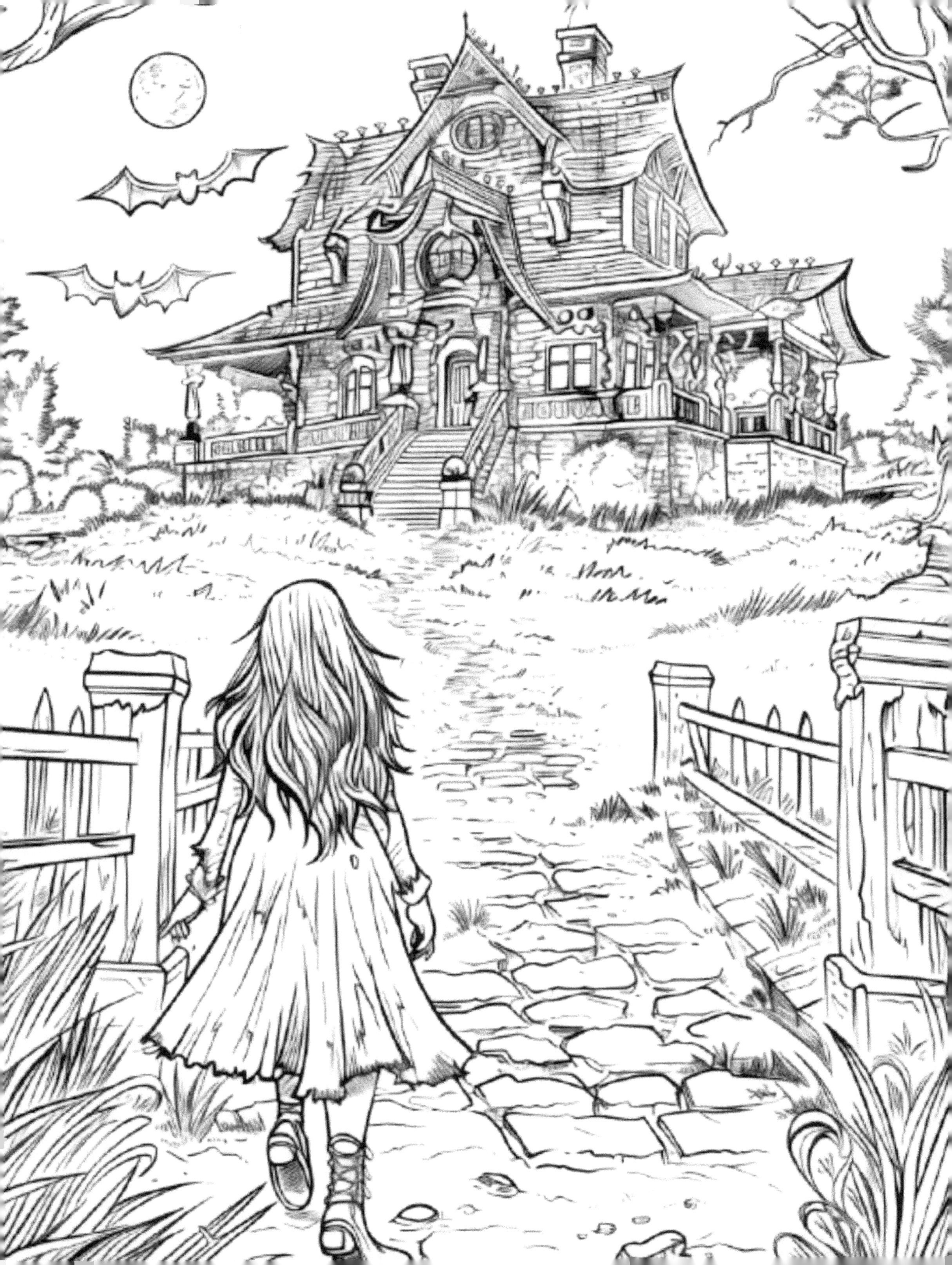

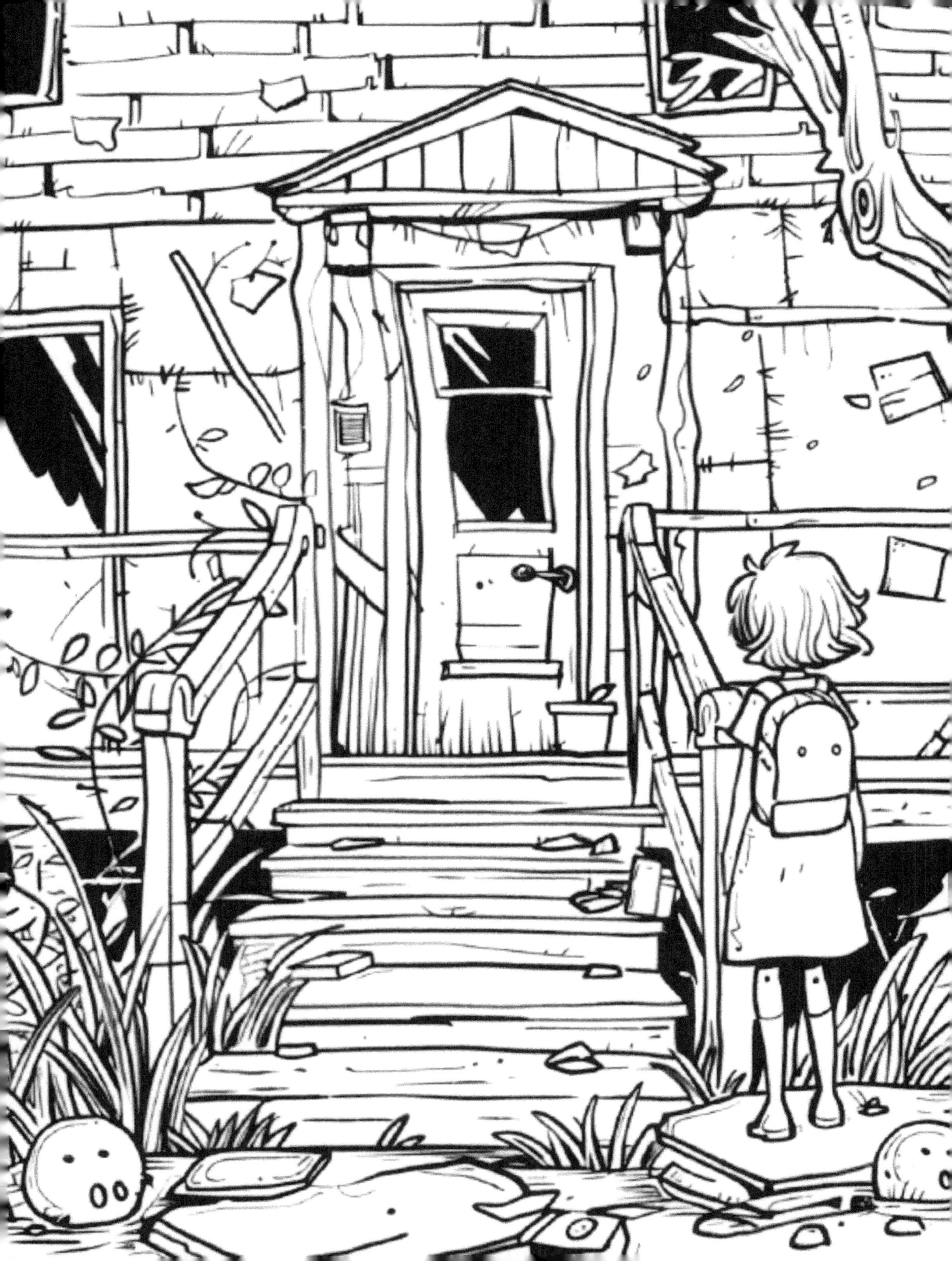

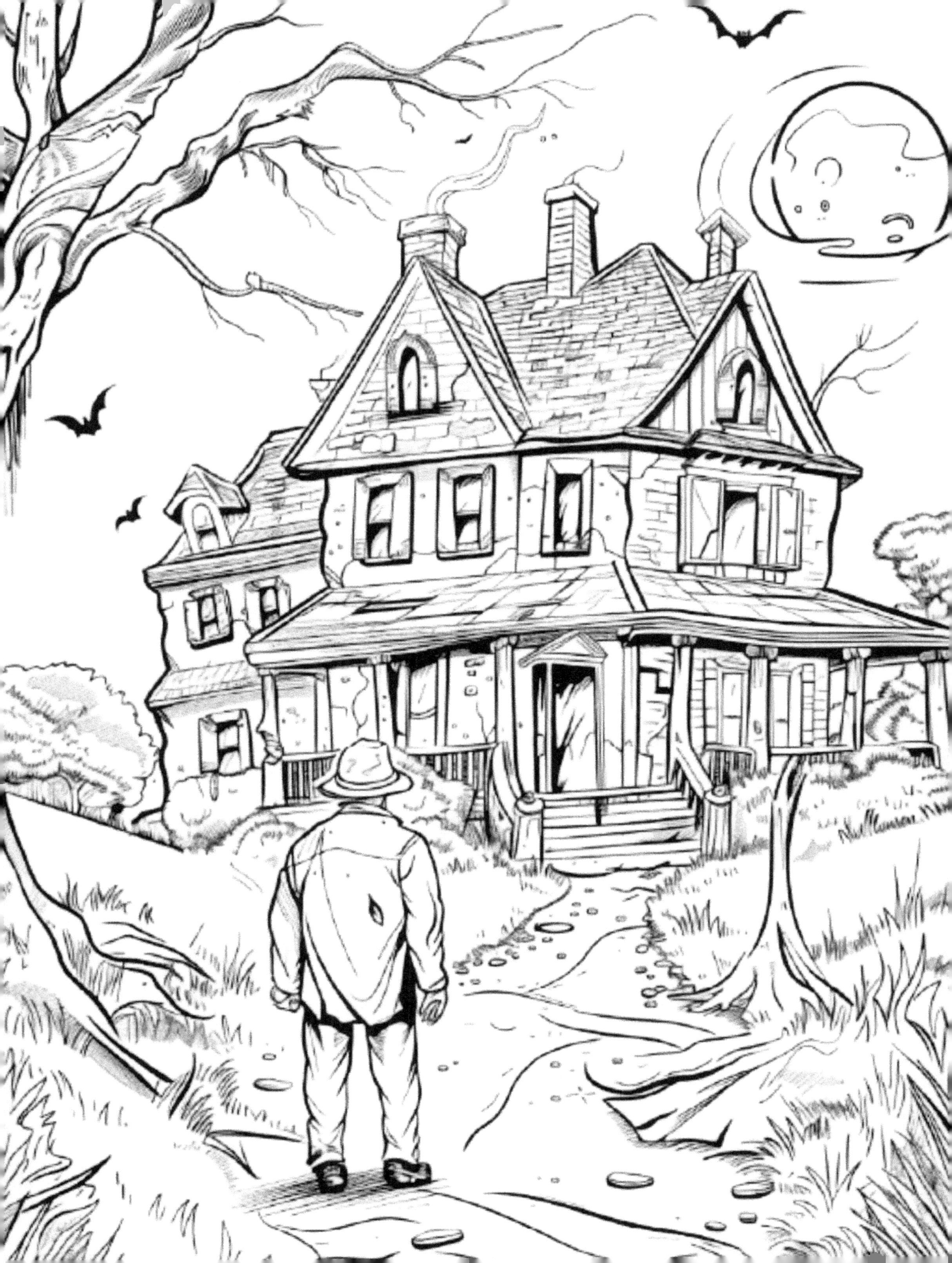

The End